13 Colonies

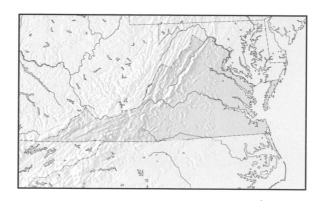

VIRGINIA

13 Colonies

VIRGINIA

THE HISTORY OF VIRGINIA COLONY, 1607–1776

ROBERTA WIENER AND JAMES R. ARNOLD

Raintree

Chicago, Illinois

For information, address the publisher:
Raintree, 100 N. LaSalle, Suite 1200, Chicago, IL 60602

Printed in China by South China Printing.
09 08 07 06 05
10 9 8 7 6 5 4 3 2 1

Library of Congress Cataloging-in-Publication Data
Wiener, Roberta, 1952-
  Virginia / Roberta Wiener and James R. Arnold.
      p. cm. -- (13 colonies)
Summary: A detailed look at the formation of the colony of Virginia, its government, and its overall history, plus a prologue on world events in 1607.
Includes bibliographical references and index.
  ISBN 0-7398-6889-6 (lib. bdg.) -- ISBN 1-4109-0313-3 (pbk.) 1. Virginia--History--Colonial period, ca. 1600-1775--Juvenile literature. 2. Virginia--History--Revolution, 1775-1783--Juvenile literature. [1. Virginia--History--Colonial period, ca. 1600-1775. 2. Virginia--History--Revolution, 1775-1783.] I. Arnold, James R. II. Title. III. Series: Wiener, Roberta, 1952-   13 colonies.
  F229.W64 2004
  975.5'02--dc21
                              2003011200

Every effort has been made to contact copyright holders of any material reproduced in this book. Any omissions will be rectified in subsequent printings if notice is given to the publishers.

Disclaimer
All the Internet addresses (URLs) given in this book were valid at the time of going to press. However, due to the dynamic nature of the Internet, some addresses may have changed, or sites may have changed or ceased to exist since publication. While the author and publishers regret any inconvenience this may cause readers, no responsibility for any such changes can be accepted by either the author or the publishers.

The paper used to print this book comes from sustainable resources.

Some words are shown in bold, **like this.** You can find out what they mean by looking in the glossary.

Title page picture: Tobacco farming in colonial Virginia.

Opposite: An artist's view of Jamestown in the 17th century.

The authors wish to thank Walter Kossmann, whose knowledge, patience, and ability to ask all the right questions have made this a better series.

PICTURE ACKNOWLEDGMENTS

AUTHORS: 18-19 COLONIAL WILLIAMSBURG FOUNDATION: 7, 11, 12, 38, 39, 47 top right, 47 bottom left LIBRARY OF CONGRESS: 9, 15, 16, 20, 21, 23, 25, 27, 28, 29, 34, 35, 36, 37, 40, 44, 46, 47 top left, 47 bottom right, 50, 54, 55, 58 NATIONAL ARCHIVES: 48, 49, 51, 56, 57 NATIONAL GUARD BUREAU: 52-53 [Twenty Brave Men, a National Guard Heritage painting by Jackson Walker] NATIONAL MARITIME MUSEUM, GREENWICH, ENGLAND: 8 NATIONAL PARK SERVICE, COLONIAL NATIONAL HISTORICAL PARK: Cover, title page, 5, 13, 22-23, 24, 26, 30-31, 32-33, 42-43 COURTESY OF THE NORTH CAROLINA OFFICE OF ARCHIVES AND HISTORY: 17

Contents

PROLOGUE: A BIRD'S-EYE VIEW OF THE WORLD IN 1607

NAVIGATION: THE SCIENCE OF FIGURING OUT ONE'S POSITION AND DIRECTION WHEN TRAVELING ON THE OCEAN

In 1607, the year Englishmen first came to Jamestown, Virginia, Europe had enjoyed more than 150 years of invention and discovery. The German invention of the printing press began the rapid spread of knowledge. The invention of better firearms changed the nature of war. Advances in **navigation** and the building of larger and better sailing ships made longer voyages possible. So the Europeans began to look outward, but they did not yet understand everything they saw.

Great seamen from Portugal were the first, since the Vikings 500 years earlier, to sail to many places that Europeans had never gone before. During the 1400s and 1500s, they reached Africa, India, the Pacific Ocean, China, and Japan. They encountered kingdoms and civilizations that had existed for centuries. Everywhere they found rulers struggling to expand their kingdoms.

A flock of birds flying eastward from Europe to Asia would have first seen the Turks. They had conquered a huge **empire** that encompassed much of Eastern Europe, the Middle East, and North Africa. This flock would then have seen that the Russians had just conquered and annexed Siberia. Flying east, the flock would come to China. Here was a land of about 60 million people, long ruled from Beijing by the Ming **dynasty**. China was in decline but still looking for opportunities to conquer and expand. Conflict raged along China's borders, particularly with the Koreans and the Japanese. Continuing east, the flock would have crossed the water to Japan. Japan was recently unified under a single conqueror and had begun trading with Europeans for the first time.

EMPIRE: ALL THE COLONIES UNDER THE CONTROL OF ONE NATION

DYNASTY: A SERIES OF RULERS FROM THE SAME FAMILY, WHO PASS THE THRONE FROM ONE FAMILY MEMBER TO ANOTHER

Had the flock then turned about over the Pacific Ocean and flown back west, they would have seen India. India was a great land of 100 million people, recently united under the rule of the conqueror, Akbar the Great. Turning to the southwest, they would have found Africa. On the African coasts were small kingdoms and several great empires, often at war and often changing leadership. The interior of Africa remained unknown to outsiders.

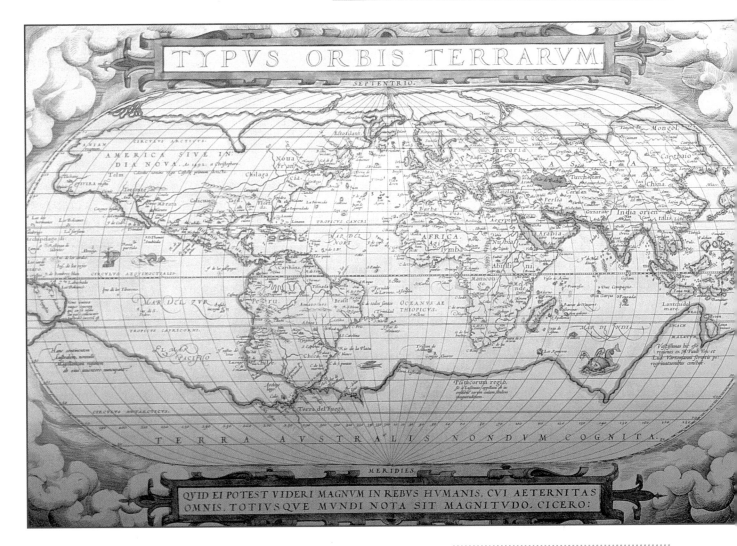

TYPVS ORBIS TERRARVM.

QVID EI POTEST VIDERI MAGNVM IN REBVS HVMANIS, CVI AETERNITAS OMNIS, TOTIVSQVE MVNDI NOTA SIT MAGNITVDO. CICERO:

The world according to a European mapmaker around 1570

Europeans did not yet have a clear idea where all these lands lay. But the Portuguese and other Europeans knew enough to see great opportunity. They saw the chance to grow rich from trade in exotic spices. They saw souls they wanted to convert to Christianity. They saw the chance to make conquests of their own and expand their countries into great empires. And not least, they saw the darker-skinned people of Africa and, thinking them a different species, they saw the chance to capture slaves.

The voyages from Europe to these distant shores were long and dangerous. Explorers had to sail from Europe all the way around Africa. So, European explorers began to sail westward in search of shortcuts. On one such voyage, in 1492, Christopher Columbus landed on an island on the far side of the Atlantic Ocean and claimed it for Spain.

NEW WORLD: THE WESTERN HEMISPHERE OF THE EARTH, INCLUDING NORTH AMERICA, CENTRAL AMERICA, AND SOUTH AMERICA; SO CALLED BECAUSE THE PEOPLE OF THE OLD WORLD, IN THE EAST, DID NOT KNOW ABOUT THE EXISTENCE OF THE AMERICAS UNTIL THE 1400S

AMERICA: LAND THAT CONTAINS THE CONTINENTS OF NORTH AMERICA AND SOUTH AMERICA

COLONY: LAND OWNED AND CONTROLLED BY A DISTANT NATION; A COLONIST IS A PERMANENT SETTLER OF A COLONY

Christopher Columbus claiming land for Spain.

He thought that he had actually sailed clear around the world and come to an island near India. Years of exploration by numerous sailors would pass before the people of Europe realized that Columbus had been the first European of their era to set foot in a land unknown to them. They called this land the **New World**, although it was not new to the people who lived there.

After Columbus, Amerigo Vespucci claimed to have reached the New World. Whether he actually did or not, a mapmaker put his name on a map in 1507, and the New World became **America**, or the Americas. Still looking for that shortcut to the riches of Asia, explorers from Spain, France, and England continued to sail to North and South America. They began to claim large pieces of these lands for their own nations.

By the time the English came to Jamestown, Jacques Cartier had claimed land for a French **colony** in Canada, and Samuel de Champlain had established a second colony on the Atlantic coast of Canada. Far to the south, French Protestants had tried to start a colony in Florida.

But the Spanish were far ahead of other Europeans in the competition for land in the Americas. Before the English came to Jamestown, the Spanish had already claimed huge portions of both North and South America for Spain. They had conquered two mighty **Native American** empires—the Aztecs and Incas. The Spanish had introduced the first domestic cattle and horses to the Americas. They had brought European civilization along with European diseases, military techniques, and weapons.

Yet there remained many places in this newly explored land where no Europeans had yet settled. All of Europe saw America not just as a possible shortcut to somewhere else, but also as a huge empty land with riches waiting to be taken. The fact that Native Americans had lived in America for more than ten thousand years did not trouble them in their thinking.

I.
THE GENTLEMEN OF THE VIRGINIA COMPANY

England lagged well behind Spain in the contest for the riches of America. In addition, England and Spain were enemies. Between 1577 and 1585, the English Admiral Sir Francis Drake had sailed around the world,

Sir Walter Raleigh sponsored far more voyages than he actually made. This picture shows him on the coast of Virginia but he never actually set foot there.

explored parts of America, attacked Spanish ships and settlements, and burned Spain's colony at St. Augustine, Florida. In 1588, Spain had sent a large fleet of ships, the famous Armada, to attack England, but the fleet was destroyed by storms and by English warships.

In the meantime, Englishman Sir Humphrey Gilbert had made several voyages in the effort to set up a trading post in North America. He was lost at sea in 1583. His **patent**, or royal permission, to explore and trade in America, passed to his half brother, Walter Raleigh.

In the spring and summer of 1584, two English ships went on a voyage sponsored by Walter Raleigh. They explored a small part of the coast of North America, the part that became present-day North Carolina. It was a beautiful time of year, with warm weather and plenty of food. The men returned to England with tempting descriptions of friendly native people, good hunting and fishing, and plentiful crops of corn and vegetables. Raleigh called the land Virginia, in honor of Queen Elizabeth I, who was known as the Virgin Queen because she never married. In return, she made Walter Raleigh a knight, and from then on he was known as Sir Walter Raleigh.

The settlers that Raleigh sent to establish a colony in America landed in what is now North Carolina. The first group gave up and returned to England. The second group disappeared without a trace, and their settlement became known as the Lost Colony. [The story of the Lost Colony is told in the book about North Carolina.] Many months went by before people in England realized that Raleigh's colony had met with a mysterious end. Meanwhile, returning explorers—along with several Native Americans they brought back to England—continued to publicize the wonders and riches of America and encourage people to go to live there. They brought back ships full of furs and told of abundant fish and thick forests full of valuable, tall trees.

Queen Elizabeth died in 1603, and James I, her distant cousin, became king of England. King James sought peace with Spain, so the Spanish persuaded him to lock up Sir Walter Raleigh, whom they considered a dangerous enemy. Other Englishmen took over the drive to reap the rewards of America.

> PATENT: OFFICIAL DOCUMENT GIVING SOMEONE THE RIGHT TO USE A PIECE OF LAND OR PERMISSION TO CONDUCT A BUSINESS

A group of men asked the king for permission to colonize the rich land known as Virginia. The king granted them a **charter** in 1606, permitting them to form a trading company and settle there. The new company, called the Virginia Company of London, included "certain Knights, gentlemen, merchants, and adventurers, of our city of London and elsewhere." These men wanted mainly to make money for themselves and the company's shareholders. The first English settlers of Virginia were trying to find gold and other valuable products to sell in England, and to search for a waterway that would serve as a shortcut to the Pacific Ocean.

CHARTER: A DOCUMENT CONTAINING THE RULES FOR RUNNING AN ORGANIZATION

John Smith, an important leader of the first English colony at Jamestown, made remarkably accurate maps of Virginia and the other places he explored.

Shipwreck!

Colonists risked much to reach the New World. Consider the voyage of the *Virginia Merchant*, which sailed from England in October 1649. When the ship was almost within sight of its goal, ill winds blew her away from the North Carolina coast and out to sea. Then, gale force winds broke two masts, leaving the ship nearly helpless and without sails. Waves washed over the deck:

> *"The ship stood stock still, with her head under water, seeming to bore her way into the sea. My two comrades and myself lay on our platform, sharing liberally in the general consternation. We took short leave of each other, men, women, and children. All assaulted with fresh terror of death, made a most dolorous outcry throughout the ship … ."*

The Sea Venture, commanded by Captain Christopher Newport, was wrecked by a storm as she carried new settlers to Virginia in 1609. This shipwreck supplied William Shakespeare with the idea for his play, "The Tempest." The shipwrecked crew and passengers spent almost a year on the island of Bermuda building two small ships to carry them to Virginia.

Waves swept several seamen overboard and caused a gaping hole. Carpenters from among the passengers frantically patched the leak. Passengers also took turns at the unending task of pumping water out of the ship. The ordeal stretched out to more than three months with the ship unable to approach the shore. The food supply ran out and the crew and passengers resorted to eating rats. At least one person starved to death. Finally, in January 1650, the *Virginia Merchant* reached the coast some distance from the English settlements, and the settlers had to go the rest of the way on foot.

2.
THE ATLANTIC VOYAGE

WEST INDIES: ISLANDS OF
THE CARIBBEAN SEA, SO
CALLED BECAUSE THE FIRST
EUROPEAN
VISITORS THOUGHT THEY
WERE NEAR INDIA

SHIP'S BISCUIT: HARD
BISCUITS THAT DON'T SPOIL
EASILY, TAKEN ON LONG
VOYAGES

Three ships, the *Godspeed, Susan Constant,* and *Discovery,* set sail from London on December 20, 1606. The ships carried 104 men and boys. Among them was John Smith, who would later become more famous than all the rest. But he spent most of this voyage under arrest because the other leaders didn't trust him. The voyagers expected to live four weeks aboard ship before landing in the **West Indies** to take on fresh food and water. Until then, they had only gruel, hard **ship's biscuit**, salted meat, and salted fish to eat. The voyage turned out far worse. Storms and opposing winds prevented all progress for six weeks. Difficult conditions continued through the four-month voyage. They did not reach Virginia until April 26, 1607.

This experience was typical. A voyage across the Atlantic in the 1600s took six or eight weeks under good conditions and much longer in stormy seas. Colonists shared their cramped and airless quarters below decks with their livestock and their possessions. They endured poor food, seasickness, and diseases caused by filthy conditions.

The route that the first Virginia colonists followed across the Atlantic curved to the south instead of going in a straight line, because the sailors were following the westerly ocean currents.

3.
VIRGINIA IN 1607

Before Europeans came to North America, trees covered most of the land. The trees grew so densely that it was said a squirrel could travel from the Atlantic coastline to the Mississippi River without having to touch the ground. Modern scientists call these woods the Eastern Deciduous Forest. (Deciduous means that the tree sheds its leaves in the autumn and grows new ones in the spring.) The two most common types of trees in the Eastern Deciduous Forest of the 17th century were oak and hickory.

The land includes three regions. The Coastal Plain lies along the Atlantic Ocean and extends inland to the fall line, or the place where the rivers fall rapidly from higher ground onto the flatter plain. Many large rivers divide the

Virginia natural features

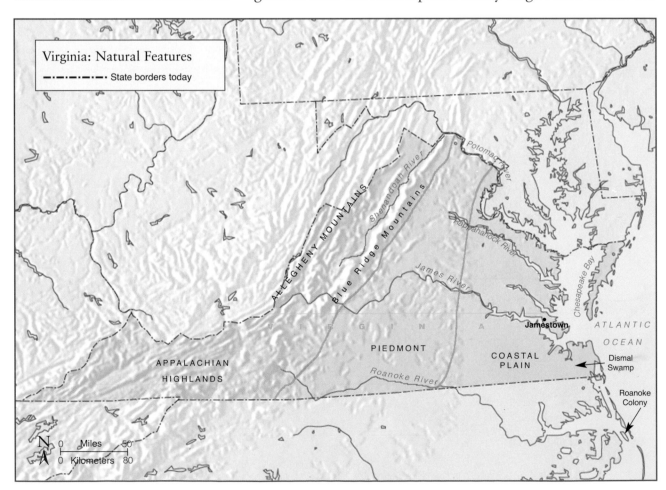

Coastal Plain. In the middle of Virginia is the Piedmont, an area of rolling hills. To the west are two mountain ranges, the Blue Ridge and the Allegheny, with the Shenandoah Valley between them.

The climate depends on elevation and closeness to saltwater. The coastal plain is usually hot and humid in the summer with temperatures sometimes over 100°F (38°C). In the winter the temperature seldom falls as low as 15°F (–10°C) and more often stays around 40 degrees. These temperatures allow an eight-month-long growing season. Farther west, summers are not so hot and winters are much colder. Everywhere there is usually ample rain to support the growth of food crops.

Three major linguistic and ethnic Native American groups lived in Virginia. They had lived in eastern North America for thousands of years. Algonquian speakers lived in the Coastal Plain's tidewater region. People speaking Iroquoian languages lived on the inner Coastal Plain and in the mountains. Siouan-speaking people occupied the Piedmont. Despite their different languages, these native peoples shared several characteristics. The most important was that they grew corn.

The native peoples lived in permanent villages. Near their homes they prepared large fields for farming. They made small mounds within these fields where they planted corn along with squash and beans. Together, these crops provided a stable food base. The Native Americans built storage places, either above or below ground, to preserve their food from one harvest until the next. They used wild foods, such as nuts and berries, to supplement what they grew. They also grew tobacco to use in their ceremonies.

Virginia was rich with wildlife. The tidal rivers, especially the Chesapeake Bay, had tremendous amounts

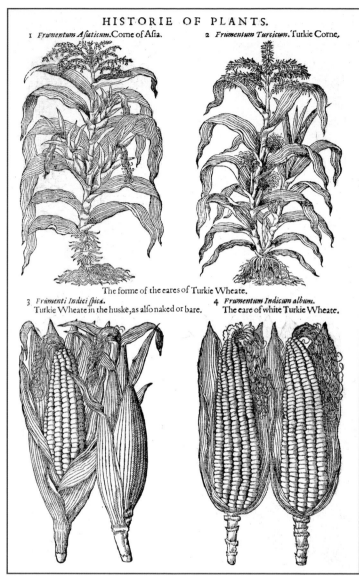

Corn was unknown to Europeans before they explored the New World. Tobacco, potatoes, tomatoes, and chocolate also originated in the New World.

During the summer Virginia's native people stayed in their villages. Women tended the fields, which the men had cleared. They built their houses of bark and woven mats placed over a framework of poles. They usually managed to grow or find just enough food to survive.

Native Americans fishing, as drawn
by an English colonist

of fin fish and shellfish. Native Americans living near the
water caught and ate fish, blue crabs, oysters, and clams.
Huge populations of waterfowl such as ducks and geese
lived in the coastal marshes. The inland forests gave food
and shelter to large populations of wild animals. Many
were useful to humans. Otters, beavers, and minks
provided valuable fur. Rabbits, deer, and game birds such
as doves and quail provided food. There were even large
herds of bison living in the western areas along the
Shenandoah River.

Before the Europeans arrived, the Native Americans

Large herds of bison, or buffalo, resembling this modern-day western herd once roamed the Shenandoah Valley of Virginia. Bison had disappeared from Virginia by the 1730s because settlers hunted and killed them for meat.

had already changed the landscape to make travel easier and to help them find food. They traveled on foot to hunt, forage, trade, and fight. By passing back and forth they wore trails into the ground. One of the greatest trails of them all, the Great Indian Warpath, went the entire length of what would become the Virginia colony from present-day Bristol north through Winchester.

The native peoples living in Virginia also set fires to make clearings in the forest for their villages and fields. They had only stone or wooden tools, so fire was the best way to take down trees. The fires burned off vegetation but left the soil intact. New plants replaced what was there before. The new plants included berries, edible roots, nuts, and fruit that provided food for the Native Americans. They also hunted the deer that came to the burned areas to feed. By the time the English arrived, some large areas had been cleared by Native Americans.

When the first English settlers arrived in 1607, eastern Virginia held about 20,000 Algonquian-speaking Native Americans. They lived in about thirty villages and accepted the rule of the great chief Powhatan. But there were not enough native peoples to create huge changes in the ecological balance.

EUROPEAN IMPACT

The arrival of the Europeans changed the ecological balance. The colonists brought with them animals and plants that were new to North America. Some of these they brought on purpose; horses, sheep, honeybees, wheat, grapevines. They brought others by accident including rats, weeds, and disease. When the new species came in contact with native species, some of the new species changed the environment.

For example, the weeds brought by accident grew rapidly and spread quickly. Weeds like dandelions and thistles were able to out-compete the native plants. All of them grew well around cleared land. So when a colonizer cleared land for his home and to plant crops, he created a place where native plants could not live and European weeds grew happily. When native plants died off, wildlife that depended upon these plants either moved away or also died.

But the biggest changes came from the European rats and from new diseases. The European rats were larger and more aggressive than the native rats. They escaped from the colonists' ships onto land. They reproduced quickly and spread inland where

The English were amazed at the appearance of the Indians. John Smith wrote about the way Indian men painted themselves: "He is the most gallant that is the most monstrous to behold."

they destroyed crops and more importantly ate the food that the Native Americans had stored to survive on through the winter.

The Europeans accidentally brought new diseases to Virginia. The most common were smallpox, measles, chicken pox, scarlet fever, typhus, influenza, whooping cough, diphtheria, and bubonic plague. These diseases had attacked Europeans for one generation after another. Over time, Europeans had developed some immunity to the germs and viruses. But the Native Americans had never been exposed to these diseases and had no immunity.

The diseases killed the Native Americans in large numbers. There are no good records of how many native people died from European diseases. However, of the approximately 20,000 Native Americans living in eastern Virginia at the time the English founded Jamestown, only 4,000 lived there 40 years later. This decline suggests how badly the native peoples of Virginia suffered from the new diseases.

The first ships carrying English colonists sail up the James River.

The Jamestown colonists' first task was to unload the ships. Among the cargo they brought with them: clothing, fabric for bedding, bushels of wheat, oil, vinegar, armor, muskets, swords, gunpowder, lead for shot, shoes, axes, saws, hammers, shovels, nails, pots, kettles, skillets, wooden dishes, and spoons.

4.
THE PERILOUS BEGINNING

The three ships of the Virginia Company entered the Chesapeake Bay on April 26, 1607. The new arrivals began looking for a place to set up their colony. They found a river that they named the James, after the king.

STOCKADE: A SERIES OF WOODEN POSTS SET INTO THE GROUND, FORMING A HIGH WALL TO PROTECT A SETTLEMENT

On May 13 they chose a site on its bank where they would live, and called it Jamestown.

These first 104 settlers, "gentlemen," and "adventurers," included shareholders, or co-owners of the Virginia Company, who would get rich if the colony did well, and company employees who were to receive only their meager pay regardless of how the company did. At least 59 of the men considered themselves to be gentlemen.

To be a gentleman in 1607 meant that one was not expected to work with one's own hands. The gentlemen of the Virginia Company came to America to find wealth. They expected Captain Christopher Newport, commander of the ships that had carried them to Jamestown, to sail back to England, pick up some working men, and bring the workers back to the colony to build houses, clear land, and plant food. Yet their difficult voyage had delayed their own arrival until late spring, and the time had nearly passed for planting.

Aside from erecting a **stockade** and a few crude shacks, nobody was volunteering to do any work, and nobody had enough authority to make them do it. In fact, few of the men, if any, actually knew how to build houses, grow food, fish, or hunt. Two months went by without anything getting done that would help the men survive. Instead, they went looking for gold, and fought among themselves about who was in charge. They ate up all the food they had taken from the ships and traded their possessions for meat and corn from the Native Americans. Without food from

Above: Captain John Smith, explorer and leader of Virginia colony. He wrote, "Virginia doth afford many excellent vegetables and living creatures, yet grass there is little or none but what groweth in low marshes: for all the country is overgrown with trees"

the native peoples they all would have starved to death. As it was, dozens died of disease and hunger.

Seven men had been appointed to the council that was to govern Virginia. Two of them were Edward Maria Wingfield, the first president of the council, and Captain John Smith. Wingfield was one of the gentlemen who had obtained the royal charter for the Virginia Company. Smith was a former army captain. The two men did not get along, because they were members of different social classes, and social class was very important in England.

Wingfield had had Smith locked up during the voyage. After landing at Jamestown, Smith went off to explore the surrounding country. A few months later, the rest of the council turned against Wingfield and replaced him with John Ratcliffe as president.

In the autumn of 1608, Smith returned from one of his

Native Americans watch the new arrivals, unsure of what the future will bring. Less than a hundred years later, an Englishman would write, "The Indians of Virginia are almost wasted … ."

Desperate Crime and Cruel Punishment

The first settlers of Jamestown lived in a violent and brutal time. Even though the settlers relied on the Native Americans for food, the settlers terrorized them because they believed the Indians would be even more cooperative if they were thoroughly frightened. In 1610, the English massacred one native village in order to terrify the others. For the same purpose, they also captured and killed the wife and children of a local chief.

The English were almost as cruel to one another. When a hungry Englishman stole food, the councilmen made an example of him. They kept him chained to a tree until he starved to death. When a group of desperate colonists ran away to the Native Americans, the other colon-ists recaptured and killed the runaways, by shooting, hanging, burning at the stake, or torture.

expeditions to find the settlers ready to overthrow Ratcliffe. So John Smith went from prisoner to president of the Jamestown colony in less than two years. His uneasy friendship with Powhatan, the chief of thirty neighboring Algonquian tribes, allowed the colonists to keep trading with the Native Americans for food. Around the same time, Captain Newport returned from England with 70 new settlers, including two women and some skilled workers. He also brought a crown, a royal robe, and other gifts for Powhatan in order to cement the alliance between the Jamestown colony and the Native Americans.

As president, Smith forced the settlers to get to work

building houses, strengthening the stockade around the settlement, clearing land, and planting crops. After months of hunger and sickness had killed off more than half of the settlers, the survivors were finally ready to listen to someone in authority. But their troubles were far from over.

The English government sent seven ships with several hundred more settlers. They arrived in 1609. Smith had been injured in an accident and left Jamestown on the return voyage. George Percy, the man who replaced Smith as council president, lacked Smith's leadership ability. The hard winter of 1609–1610 is known as the "starving time." The more than 200 Jamestown settlers ate all of their livestock, their cats and dogs, and rats and mice. One man killed his wife with the intention of eating her body. For his crime he was burned at the stake. Some men left the colony in search of food and never returned. Most starved to death. By spring, at least three people out of four had died or disappeared.

In May 1610 Captain Newport, delayed almost a year by a shipwreck, arrived to find the survivors, about 60 people, ready to give up and return to England. Just as

"The sixth of August there died John Asbie … The ninth day died George Flowre of the swelling. The tenth day died William Bruster Gentleman, of a wound given by the savages, and was buried the eleventh day. The fourteenth day Jerome Alicock Ancient, died of a wound, the same day Francis Midwinter, Edward Moris Corporal died suddenly. The fifteenth day, there died …" So wrote one of the first English colonists, truthfully, about life and death in Jamestown.

Captain John Smith's Adventures in North America

1607–1608: *John Smith left Jamestown frequently to trade with the native peoples for food. On one trip he went far up the Chickahominy River in search of a passage to the Pacific Ocean. A group of Native Americans captured him, killed his companions, and held him captive for several weeks. According to Smith, his captors were about to execute him when Chief Powhatan's 11-year-old daughter, Pocahontas, saved him. Smith reported that Pocahontas threw herself down next to him, placed her head next to his, and pleaded for his life. Powhatan spared his life, called him a friend and, a few days later, released him. Whether or not the events took place exactly as Smith described them, Pocahontas became a frequent visitor to Jamestown after Smith's release. Some historians think that the mock execution was actually a ceremony adopting Smith into the tribe.*

This is a highly romanticized image of the rescue of John Smith. Pocahontas is shown as a beautiful woman, rather than the 11-year-old girl she was. The feather headdress of the chief was typical of the western Plains Indians of a later time.

Summer 1608: *Smith and a party of settlers explored the Chesapeake Bay and found the mouth of the Potomac River. Still hoping to find a passage to the Pacific, they pushed up the river until they came to the rapids at Great Falls. Forced to turn back, they returned to Jamestown. Smith found he was selected to be president of the governing council. He drew an accurate map of the region based on his many trading and exploring trips.*

1614: *A group of English merchants paid for John Smith to lead an expedition to the New England coast. He was supposed to look for gold, trade for furs, and catch fish and whales. He did succeed in returning with fish and furs, but his most important achievement was his very accurate map of the coast.*

1615: *Smith set sail again for the New World but was captured at sea by French pirates. By the time he escaped three months later and returned to England, he had lost everything he owned. He was never again able to cross the Atlantic Ocean.*

Smith taketh the King of Pamavnkee prifoner 1608

Smith was the only English witness to his adventures, which have passed into legend. He was born in England in 1580, the son of a tenant farmer [one who does not own the land he farms]. John Smith became the apprentice of a prosperous merchant. Seeking adventure, Smith became a soldier at the age of 20 and went off to fight in a war against the Turks. After he left North America for the last time, he wrote a book about Virginia. It was well received and remains an important source of information. John Smith died in 1631.

Indentured Servitude

The establishment of colonies in North America served the interests of Great Britain by giving the nation a foothold on the other side of the Atlantic Ocean. Those who settled the British colonies in North America were the foot soldiers of England's battle for empire. They put their lives at risk for a chance to own land and gain personal wealth, which was something they could never hope to have in England.

Men of the upper classes also were attracted to Virginia because they could establish a successful tobacco plantation and thus gain greater wealth and more land than they could have in England. They could cheaply purchase the labor of indentured servants to do the work of raising tobacco. A servant bound to work four to seven years could be bought for six pounds [English money], the cost of transporting a person across the Atlantic.

In the early years of the colony, many of the indentured servants were brought to Virginia by force. Orphans, beggars, petty criminals, and unemployed or homeless people were gathered up from the streets and bundled aboard ships, to be sold into servitude across the ocean. Later, as people learned of the opportunity to gain land and prosper, many chose to accept servitude as a way to get to Virginia. People who might only hope to be servants in England gambled on the chance to be landowners and independent farmers in Virginia.

Three out of four immigrants to Virginia in the 1600s arrived as indentured

In England, only landowners were allowed to hunt and fish. Anyone else was considered a criminal. Colonists from the non-landowning class treasured the right to hunt and fish as they pleased in Virginia.

servants. During their servitude, they received only food, clothing, and shelter. On earning their freedom, they were supposed to receive from their masters food, clothing, and tools with which to make a fresh start. In addition, freed male servants in Virginia received 50 acres of land. The women, who made up about ten percent of the indentured servants, got the chance to marry a man who owned some land.

From 1607 to 1622, more than 10,000 people sailed to Virginia, yet only 2,000 colonists still lived there in 1622. Four out of five had died in the colony's first 15 years. Diseases, attacks by native peoples, and overwork by harsh masters raised the death toll. Colonial laws tended to favor the master over the servant, so that masters who beat or killed their servants were not punished. The upper-class men in government believed that beatings were necessary to keep the servants in line. They also punished servants who escaped by adding time to the length of servitude.

As Jamestown grew, its defensive stockade and the water surrounding it remained essential to the colonists' safety from attack. However, the location, near so much water, also bred disease-carrying mosquitos.

they were about to sail, three ships arrived carrying new settlers, plentiful food, and Thomas West, Lord De la Warr, the colony's newly appointed governor. Like Smith, Lord De la Warr put the colonists to work.

Still, many colonists died of malaria and typhoid fever. Jamestown was in a swampy location where malaria-bearing mosquitos bred. The settlers caught typhoid because they relied on the sluggish river for drinking water while heedlessly polluting it with their own sewage. Other settlers were occasionally killed by Native Americans when they went outside the walls of the town. The population of Jamestown again fell sharply.

Illness forced Lord De la Warr to return to England. His deputies, Sir Thomas Dale and Sir Thomas Gates, both veteran soldiers, placed the colony under strict rule. They required, among other things, that all colonists attend church. The colony survived but did not find riches as the founders of the Virginia Company had hoped. In England the Virginia Company tried selling shares of stock, and even lottery tickets, to make enough money to keep the company going.

TRIUMPH OF TOBACCO

Then John Rolfe, a settler who had arrived in 1609, put the Jamestown colony on a new path. He wanted to grow tobacco so he would always have enough to smoke. The Native Americans' tobacco was a bitter type, but Rolfe planted some seeds of a milder West Indian tobacco. He grew his first crop in 1612, and two years later had enough to send to England for sale. Soon all the colonists wanted to grow tobacco. It was easy to grow and easily sold for a high price.

The Virginia Company began offering free land to settlers. This offer, along with the growing reputation of tobacco as a money-making crop, attracted more and more colonists. The colony spread from Jamestown along the banks of the James River. The expansion of the colony upset the Native Americans.

One man's experiment with tobacco thus had a major effect on the history of Virginia. More settlers came to Virginia, expecting to own land, grow tobacco, and make money. In fact, tobacco came to be used as money in Virginia. Agriculture in the Virginia colony meant growing tobacco, and other crops held only a minor place.

Growing tobacco led to the establishment of large plantations worked by **indentured** servants and slaves. The first African slaves arrived in Jamestown in 1619. The rich untapped soil of Virginia at first produced abundant crops. But, as time went on, the soil wore out and lost its fertility. So the **planters** needed ever more land to keep making money from tobacco. The colonists' growing need for land, and the use of slaves to work huge plantations, later played an important role in the history of the United States.

INDENTURE: AGREEMENT TO WORK FOR SOMEONE FOR A CERTAIN NUMBER OF YEARS, IN EXCHANGE FOR FOOD, A PLACE TO SLEEP, AND PAYMENT OF ONE'S PASSAGE ACROSS THE ATLANTIC TO THE COLONIES

PLANTER: OWNER OF A PLANTATION, OR LARGE FARM

A tobacco field. King James I called smoking "loathsome to the eye, hateful to the nose, harmful to the brain, ... dangerous to the lungs." Yet tobacco had come to stay. Farmers in the southern part of the modern state of Virginia still grow tobacco.

The Short Life of Pocahontas

In 1613 an English captain tricked Pocahontas into boarding his ship, and then kept her as a hostage. He hoped to exchange her for some Englishmen captured by Powhatan. Held at Jamestown and treated kindly, she learned to speak English, agreed to convert to Christianity, and was renamed Rebecca.

At the age of 18 she married the Englishman John Rolfe, who had fallen in love with her. He also believed he was saving her soul by keeping her in Christian society. Powhatan consented to the marriage and sent Pocahontas' uncle and two brothers to attend the wedding. The wedding brought about a period of peace.

The couple and their infant son visited England in 1616, where Pocahontas, now Rebecca Rolfe, was introduced to the king and queen. Before the Rolfes could return to Virginia, she fell ill and died in 1617, at the age of 21. Her young son, Thomas Rolfe, grew up to found a long line of Virginians.

Above: This is the only portrait of Pocahontas for which she actually posed. It was painted in England.

Below: Pocahontas being introduced to King James I

A Dutch ship brought about 20 Africans to be sold as slaves in 1619. At first, Virginians preferred indentured servants because of the high death rate among the settlers. Slaves cost more than servants because they were sold for life, but they might only live a few years.

For many years, most of the Virginia settlers were men. In 1624 only one settler in six was female. The few unmarried women who crossed the Atlantic were expected to quickly become wives.

BURGESS: A CITIZEN OF A BURG OR BOROUGH; A REPRESENTATIVE ELECTED TO THE LOWER HOUSE OF THE VIRGINIA COLONIAL LEGISLATURE, CALLED THE HOUSE OF BURGESSES

After a difficult start and many deaths, it became clear that the English had come to Virginia to stay. In 1619, twelve years after the first Englishmen had arrived at Jamestown, the settlement became the site of the first English representative government in the Americas. The free, landowning men of eleven districts elected twenty-two **burgesses**. The burgesses met to pass laws to govern the colony.

MASSACRE!

By 1622 more than a thousand English men and women lived in Virginia along the James River. They had enjoyed a period of relative peace with the Native Americans, cemented by the marriage of chief Powhatan's daughter, Pocahontas, to the English colonist, John Rolfe. However, when Powhatan died in 1618, his half-brother, Opechancanough, began planning to drive the English from the land.

On a single day in March 1622, bands of Native Americans launched coordinated surprise attacks on English settlements and slaughtered every settler they could find, including women and children. Jamestown itself received warning and was able to fight off the attackers. About 350 people were killed, one colonist in three, before the settlers could organize a defense. Peaceful relations between the English colonists and Powhatan's people came to an end.

The massacre of 1622, as it came to be known, gave the colonists the justification they needed to destroy the Native Americans, whom they saw as less-than-human savages. The English took to burning Native American villages and crops just before the autumn harvest. When winter came starvation did the rest. In one deceitful episode, the English invited the native peoples to sign a treaty and poisoned those who attended. The war would continue until the Native Americans were scattered and destroyed.

In simultaneous attacks, Native Americans surprised several English settlements and slaughtered men, women, and children. The English referred to the attacks as the "Massacre of 1622."

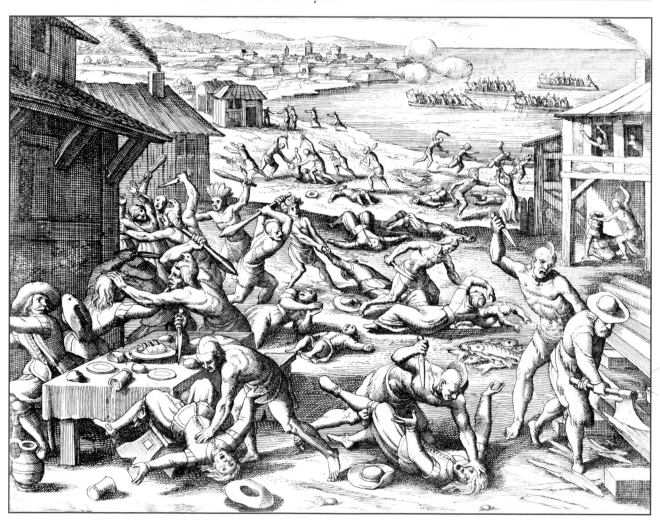

5. LIFE IN THE ROYAL COLONY

The English remained in Virginia and began to prosper, but they were not making enough money to keep the Virginia Company in business. In 1624 King James revoked, or took away, the company's charter and made Virginia a royal colony. From this time on it was to be ruled by a **royal governor**, but it did keep its elected legislature, the House of Burgesses. The burgesses made laws governing many aspects of colonial life such as how much tobacco could be produced, what could be preached in churches, and how much the settlers had to pay in **taxes**. Men in colonial government came from the wealthier landowning class. They tended to make laws that favored their wealthy peers.

One governor, William Berkeley, ruled over Virginia for many years, from 1642 to 1652, and again from 1660

Below: The English used tobacco, first brought to England in 1586, to treat headaches, kidney stones, blisters, and toothache. Young students at Eton, a famous English boarding school, were taught how to smoke tobacco in order to prevent the plague. They were whipped if they did not smoke regularly! A Virginia law attempted to prevent overproduction, which caused prices to fall: "Be it … ordered that no planter or master of a family shall plant or cause to be planted above two thousand plants … It is likewise enacted, that no person shall tend … above 14 leaves, nor gather … above 9 leaves upon a plant of tobacco …"

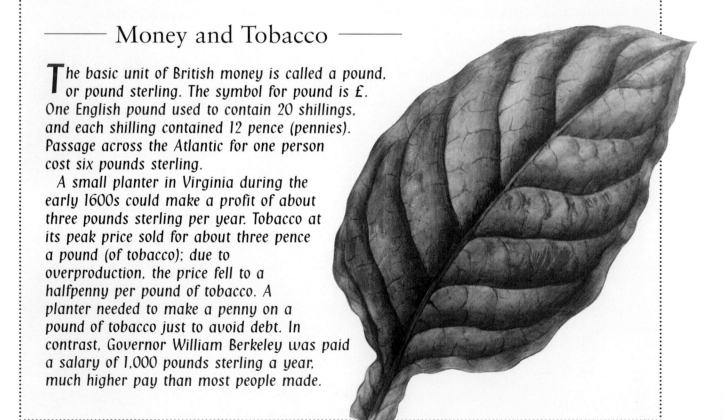

Money and Tobacco

The basic unit of British money is called a pound, or pound sterling. The symbol for pound is £. One English pound used to contain 20 shillings, and each shilling contained 12 pence (pennies). Passage across the Atlantic for one person cost six pounds sterling.

A small planter in Virginia during the early 1600s could make a profit of about three pounds sterling per year. Tobacco at its peak price sold for about three pence a pound (of tobacco); due to overproduction, the price fell to a halfpenny per pound of tobacco. A planter needed to make a penny on a pound of tobacco just to avoid debt. In contrast, Governor William Berkeley was paid a salary of 1,000 pounds sterling a year, much higher pay than most people made.

Virginia came to be called the Old Dominion because of its loyalty to King Charles II while he was in exile during the English Civil War. Led by Oliver Cromwell, the anti-royalists had executed Charles I and taken over the government of England.

Military defense was an essential function in the early Virginia settlements. Archaeologists dug up this ancient helmet near Jamestown.

to 1677. Early in Berkeley's reign, in 1644, the now old and ailing Opechancanough launched a last all-out attack on the English.

The attack came about because the wealthiest tobacco planters had bought up the best land near the coast. As their bound servants fulfilled their indentures, they had to move ever farther from Jamestown to find land. This angered the ancient chief, and he again set his warriors upon the **frontier** settlers, killing more than 400 English men, women, and children.

By 1644 the colony had grown to a population of nearly ten thousand, so the death toll of Opechancanough's last attack did not have as great an effect as that of the earlier massacre. In fact, the colonists now outnumbered the Native Americans. Exposure to European diseases and long years of warfare had reduced the Native American population of Virginia to barely half of what it had been when the first settlers arrived.

In 1646 the English finally captured Opechancanough, but before he could be transported to England, one of the settlers murdered him at Jamestown. The people of Powhatan's once-great kingdom were confined to reservations. English settlers now had the legal right to shoot them on sight if they were seen on English property. This, however, was not the end of war with Native Americans. Other native groups lived beyond the settled area, and the English, in their quest for more land, would eventually encounter them.

Another scene in the ongoing war between the Virginia colonists and the Indians.

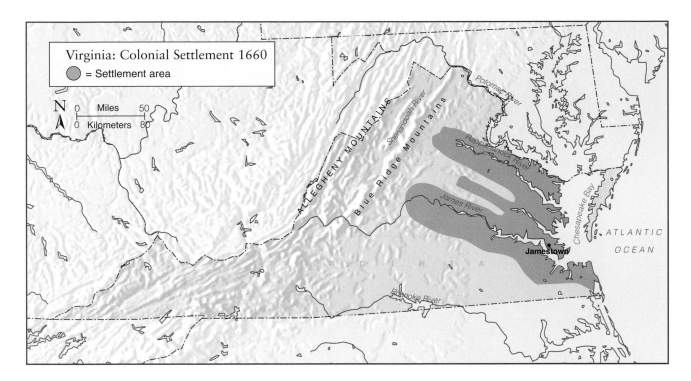

Virginia: Colonial Settlement 1660

= Settlement area

N

Miles 50

Kilometers 80

ALLEGHENY MOUNTAINS

Shenandoah River

Blue Ridge Mountains

Potomac River

Rappahannock River

James River

Chesapeake Bay

ATLANTIC OCEAN

Jamestown

Roanoke River

V I R G I N I A

The colony continued to grow, but its population increased mostly through the arrival of new settlers from the **Old World**. For the colony's first 50 years, about a quarter of all the colonists died of disease, or from being overworked during their years of servitude.

However, after the final defeat of Powhatan's people, in the mid-1600s, a servant who survived his indenture found plenty of good land available on the frontier. To live on the frontier, a farmer cleared a small part of his land for planting and left the rest wooded until declining fertility forced him to clear another field. Livestock ranged freely in the surrounding woods.

In the 1660s and 1670s, times again grew hard for the colonists. So much tobacco had been grown and shipped to England that the price fell below the cost of production. The government of England made matters worse by passing the Navigation **Acts**. These laws required colonists to ship their tobacco only on English ships to England, preventing them from selling their tobacco in any other country.

The government of Virginia also made things hard on the small planters by imposing unusually high taxes. The burgesses, most of whom Governor Berkeley had chosen

OLD WORLD: EUROPE, ASIA, AND AFRICA

ACT: LAW, SO-CALLED BECAUSE IT IS MADE BY AN ACT OF GOVERNMENT

from among his friends, voted high taxes to pay their own and the governor's salaries. Small planters paid about ten percent of their crops in taxes, while the wealthy planters paid lower taxes on their holdings and some had no taxes at all. Governor Berkeley canceled all elections starting in 1661, keeping his friends in power for fifteen years.

Berkeley gave his friends huge grants of the best land. By the mid 1660s, his favoritism shut freed servants out of landownership, so they had to become tenant farmers or move to the frontier and fight the unconquered western Native Americans for land.

In 1675 open warfare broke out between frontier settlers and the Susquehannock Indians. Berkeley did not

Nathaniel Bacon confronts Governor Berkeley .

want the frontier people to pursue the war for several reasons. His wealthy favorites had a valuable trade in deerskins with the conquered Algonquians who had once been ruled by Powhatan. They also wanted the frontier to remain a dangerous place so that freedmen would stay in the east and work for them as tenants.

BACON'S REBELLION

Nathaniel Bacon, a 29-year-old gentleman distantly related to the governor, stepped into the conflict between the wealthy planters of the coastal tidewater region and the struggling frontier dwellers. A member of the English upper class, Bacon was as concerned with getting his share of wealth and power as he was with the plight of servants and frontier farmers.

Bacon led brutal attacks on both friendly and hostile Native Americans. He also encouraged servants to desert and steal from their masters. Bacon's actions caused the governor to accuse him of treason. Bacon then marched his armed group to Jamestown and burned it to the ground as the governor fled. But the rebellion came to a standstill when Bacon suddenly fell ill and died. After Bacon's death, the governor returned to the capital and hanged 23 of Bacon's rebels, seizing their property for his friends. The authorities in London realized that Governor Berkeley had gone too far and enraged many Virginians, so England sent troops across the Atlantic and forced Berkeley to leave Virginia.

In the end, Bacon's rebellion succeeded. The burgesses reduced taxes and tried to make the government popular with the common people. They changed their policy of trading with the Native Americans and instead supported the frontier dwellers in making war on the Native Americans in the west. Berkeley's successors in the office of royal governor met resistance whenever they tried to raise taxes. Tobacco prices rose, and the Virginia government again awarded land to freed servants. Over time, relations improved between large and small planters, and the legislature came to more fairly represent the people. In contrast, the royal governor came to represent the heavy hand of distant English authority.

Above and Below: Buildings in Williamsburg. The College of William & Mary, the second oldest college in the colonies, was founded in 1693 at a place called Middle Plantation. After a fire destroyed the government building in Jamestown, the Virginia assembly met for the first time in Middle Plantation in 1699. Middle Plantation was renamed Williamsburg and the new capitol building was erected between 1701 and 1705.

How the Virginia Colonial Government Worked

The Crown (king or queen) appointed the royal governor, who had detailed instructions from the Crown and a great deal of power. The royal governor served as a stand-in for the Crown. He had the power to call the assembly into session, to give out land and favors, and to veto laws. He appointed powerful councillors from the privileged classes. The appointed council and the elected House of Burgesses formed the general assembly, which also had a lot of power in Virginia.

Local government was at first organized by church parishes, or districts, but counties gradually replaced parishes. The governor ordered elections through the county courts and sheriffs, who held elections for burgesses to represent counties. Only male landowners could vote. The counties collected taxes to pay local officials' salaries.

The county court system kept public records of indentures, livestock brands, land titles, and wills. The courts also organized the care of poor people, handled lawsuits, punished minor crimes, and ran public services such as ferries and bridges. Court officials, appointed by the governor, included justices of the peace (George Washington was one), the clerk, and the sheriff, along with their deputies.

6.
BATTLES FOR DOMINION

The decades after Bacon's Rebellion brought growing prosperity to the Virginia colonists. However, a new conflict broke out. By the 1740s, adventuresome traders from Virginia and Pennsylvania had made their way over the Allegheny mountains into the Ohio Valley. There they met with western Native Americans to trade for furs. In exchange the **British** offered guns and gunpowder, tools, rum, and other merchandise.

At the same time, French traders were operating from the north and west, entering Native American country from Canada, the Great Lakes, and the Mississippi Valley. The French and British viewed one another as competitors for Native American trade, and they also both wanted to claim the western lands for their countries. British mapmakers of the time drew the colonies' borders in straight lines all the way to the Pacific Ocean. Both the French and the British tried to get the Native Americans on their side by giving them gifts. The French traders

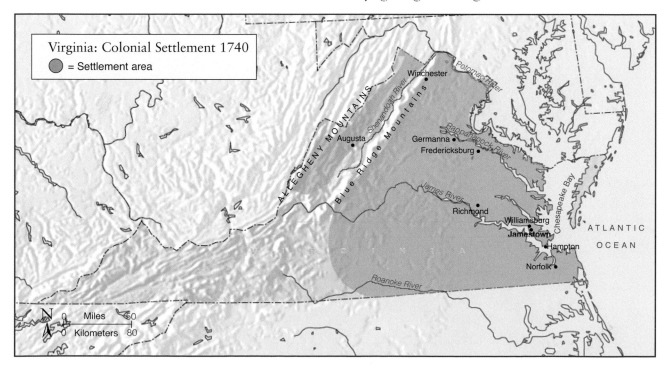

Virginia: Colonial Settlement 1740

● = Settlement area

ALLEGHENY MOUNTAINS

Blue Ridge Mountains

Potomac River

Winchester

Shenandoah River

Augusta

Germanna

Rappahannock River

Fredericksburg

James River

Richmond

Williamsburg

Jamestown

Hampton

Chesapeake Bay

ATLANTIC OCEAN

Norfolk

Roanoke River

VIRGINIA

N

Miles 50

Kilometers 80

especially got along well with their Native American trading partners. Many of them lived among the native peoples and married Native American women.

By 1750, many of the prominent planters of Virginia had used up the soil of their tidewater plantations and built new plantations in the Shenandoah valley. Less wealthy German, Irish, and Scottish farmers from the colonies to the north and south had also moved into the valley. Many looked to the Ohio country as the next source of new farmland. A group of Virginians formed the Ohio Company and got a huge land grant on the Ohio River from King George II. However, the British government paid more attention to wars in Europe than to securing new land in North America.

Neither Pennsylvania nor Virginia was willing to spend money to build forts in the disputed western territory. Then in 1752, French settlers led a troop of Native Americans from Canada in an attack on the main British trading post in Ohio country. They massacred and mutilated the outnumbered British and Native Americans at the post.

Going to Church in Williamsburg during the 1700s. The Church of England was the established church of the Virginia colony. Local governing bodies called vestries ran church affairs for each district, or parish. The Virginia state government disestablished the Church of England after the Revolution.

Right: Frontier settlers were often freed servants who, for the first time in their lives, were living on land they owned. Their furnishings and possessions were simple and their survival depended on their own hard work. The earliest houses of the colony were thatched-roof cottages like those in England. Log cabins and wood frame houses came later.

Virginia planters tried to live like the upper classes of England, with fine houses and furniture. Many plantation houses were wood frame with wood shingles. The wealthiest soon began building their houses of brick. Wrote one traveler: "The gentlemen's seats [houses] are of late built for the most part of good brick and many of timber very handsome, commodious, and capacious; and likewise the common planters live in pretty timber houses, neater than the farm houses are generally in England...."

George Washington (on horseback) watches his men raise the British flag over Fort Necessity.

The following year the French built several forts in the western part of modern-day Pennsylvania.

Governor Robert Dinwiddie of Virginia assigned a 21-year-old militiaman named George Washington to go on a difficult mission. Washington was to travel west with a small group of men, meet with the French at their outposts, inform them they were trespassing on Virginia property, and warn them to leave. He set out from the capital, Williamsburg, in October 1753 and returned in January 1754 to report that the French had no intention of leaving Ohio voluntarily. A **surveyor** from the age of 16, Washington provided one useful result of his hard journey, a good map of the country where he had traveled.

The Virginia governor sent a **militia** company west to build a British fort at the site of present-day Pittsburgh. A party of about 500 French and Native American men drove off the outnumbered Virginians, preventing them from completing the fort. Instead, the French completed it and called it Fort Duquesne.

Next, George Washington arrived with a small force of about 60 men. He was too late to defend the fort.

However, Washington heard that some French soldiers were nearby and mounted a surprise attack on them. Washington and his Virginians defeated the small group of Frenchmen. He then ordered the construction of a fort on the site, which he named Fort Necessity. But on July 3, 1754, nearly a thousand French and Native Americans attacked the fort. Washington had no choice but to surrender.

That battle started a new war between **Great Britain** and France, a long world war whose battles raged on both sides of the Atlantic Ocean. The two nations fought for control of territories in North America, the West Indies, Europe, and India. In America, the war came to be called the French and Indian War. In Europe the war was called the Seven Years' War.

The defeat at Fort Necessity got the attention of the authorities in distant Great Britain. Britain sent a large number of British soldiers to North America to fight

Above: George Washington works as a surveyor. Colonial land surveyors were county court officials.

GREAT BRITAIN: NATION FORMED BY ENGLAND, WALES, SCOTLAND, AND NORTHERN IRELAND; THE TERM "GREAT BRITAIN" CAME INTO USE WHEN ENGLAND AND SCOTLAND FORMALLY UNIFIED IN 1707

Left: George washington at his plantation, Mount Vernon, wears the elegant clothes he favored.

the French. In 1755 more than 1,000 troops landed in Virginia under the command of General Edward Braddock. Joined by George Washington and about 450 Virginia and Maryland soldiers, Braddock and his men marched straight across Virginia and into Pennsylvania, intending to retake Fort Duquesne.

As the large army of red-coated British soldiers approached the fort on a narrow wilderness path, they made an easy target for a surprise attack. On July 9, a small force of French and Indian men ambushed the army, shooting from the cover of the woods. In just three hours, they mortally wounded Braddock and killed more than 900 of his men, and lost only 43 of their own.

The wounded General Braddock was carried from the battle by his retreating soldiers. He died four days later. The ambush became known as Braddock's Defeat.

Colonel George Washington parades with his Virginia militia.

After Braddock's defeat, the surviving British **regulars** marched off to fight in New York, leaving the Virginians to defend their own frontier as best they could. The disastrous defeat had left the western frontier open to numerous and deadly Native American raids. The Native Americans burned settlers' cabins and killed their families. Colonel Washington spent the next three years commanding a regiment assigned to protect the Virginia frontier. Virginia colonists, already resentful of British royal authority, grew to resent the British even more for having failed to protect them.

REGULARS: FULL-TIME
SOLDIERS IN AN ARMY

A 1756 battle on the western Virginia frontier: 20 British settlers defeated 50 Native Indians led by a French captain.

A British tax stamp

7·
REBELLION

The rest of the French and Indian War took place to the north, in New York and in Canada. The British defeated the French at Quebec in 1759 and took control of Canada, and in 1763 France and Great Britain signed a peace treaty giving the British control of much of North America. Large numbers of new immigrants then began to arrive in the colonies from Great Britain, Germany, and other parts of Europe. That number would grow to a million over the next ten years. The war had two results that forever changed relations between Great Britain and her North American colonies.

The western Native Americans protested the arrival of even more British settlers, who occupied their land and drove away the game animals. In order to keep peace with the Native Americans, the British government issued the Proclamation of 1763. This act forbade colonists to settle any land west of the Allegheny mountains and ordered existing settlers to return east. Everybody was upset. Settlers and investors who thought they owned land now found that they did not. The government of Virginia no longer had the authority to issue grants of land west of the mountains. The British king had taken over that authority.

The war with France also convinced the British that the colonists should help pay the costs of sending soldiers to defend against Native Americans. **Parliament** imposed taxes on the colonists, and this enraged them. The first major new tax law was the Sugar Act of 1764. The act called for import and export duties, or taxes, to be paid on many trade goods, such as sugar, coffee, **indigo**, and animal hides. The British sent royal navy ships to patrol the American coast and enforce the law. They also assigned customs officials to collect the taxes and had merchants arrested who were thought to be evading the taxes.

Next, in 1765 Parliament passed the Stamp Act. Under the Stamp Act, colonists had to pay to have most documents stamped or risk arrest. Even newspapers had to have stamps. The Stamp Act affected colonists of all social classes, and resistance grew throughout the colonies. Riots broke out, and groups calling themselves the Sons of Liberty attacked the offices and homes of tax collectors.

In Virginia, Patrick Henry, a member of the House of Burgesses, led the opposition to British-imposed taxes. He made a fiery speech in the House of Burgesses, a speech that many of his peers considered treason. The legislators came to agree that resistance was necessary, and they adopted the Virginia Resolves in May 1765. The resolves stated that the local government had the right to make laws for Virginia, and that Great Britain could not impose taxes.

Patrick Henry–A Virginia Radical

Patrick Henry was born to Scottish parents on the Virginia frontier in 1736. From the age of 15 he worked as a shopkeeper and a farmer. He married at the age of 18. Needing to make more money to support his family, Henry studied to become a lawyer. As a lawyer, he showed the speaking ability that won cases and later stirred Virginians to take up arms against Great Britain.

Elected to the Virginia House of Burgesses, Henry represented and served the people of the frontier from which he had come. He and Lord Dunmore became bitter opponents as the colony moved toward revolution. When the rebels drove Dunmore from Virginia, Henry was elected governor in his place. Patrick Henry's most famous speech, which he made before the Burgesses in March 1775, ended with these words:

"Gentlemen may cry, peace, peace; but there is no peace. The war is actually begun! The next gale that sweeps from the north will bring to our ears the clash of resounding arms! Our brethren are already in the field! Why stand we here idle? What is it that gentlemen wish? What would they have? Is life so dear or peace so sweet as to be purchased at the price of chains and slavery? Forbid it, Almighty God—I know not what course others may take; but as for me, give me liberty or give me death."

March 21, 1775

The Stamp Act was so unpopular that Parliament repealed it in March 1766. Still, King George III insisted that Great Britain's Parliament had the right to make laws for the colonies and collect taxes. Parliament passed a new set of laws taxing even more products and angering more colonists. Tensions continued to grow between colonists and British soldiers and officials.

The leaders of opposition to British laws formed Committees of Correspondence throughout the colonies. By writing letters, the Committees would keep one another informed and make plans for the colonies to cooperate. They also planned to spread news that would influence public opinion in favor of rebellion. Patrick Henry and Thomas Jefferson formed the Committee of Correspondence in Virginia. The Committees got all the colonies except New Hampshire to **boycott** English merchandise. The boycott convinced the British to repeal most taxes by 1770, except for the tax on tea.

FROM BOYCOTT TO BATTLEFIELD

Relieved of tax burdens for a while, the colonies prospered, and colonial life remained calm until 1773. Few colonists really wanted independence from Great Britain, as long as they could make their own laws and set their own taxes. Then Parliament passed a law that gave one British tea seller, the struggling East India Company, special treatment. The East India Company was given a monopoly in the colonies, so that it could sell its tea more cheaply than any other dealer. Once again, the Committees of Correspondence went to work, spreading news of the new law and the coming East India Company tea shipments. The Sons of Liberty organized actions against the shipments.

The first such action, the famous Boston Tea Party, occurred in December 1773 with the dumping of a large tea shipment into Boston Harbor. Actions in other port cities followed. In 1774, Yorktown, Virginia, had a small "tea party" of its own, in which a couple of chests of tea were dumped into the York River.

When Parliament responded to the Boston Tea Party

Virginian Thomas Jefferson was born in 1743. He attended college and became a lawyer. Jefferson served as governor of Virginia during the Revolution, and became president of the United States in 1800.

BOYCOTT: AN AGREEMENT TO REFUSE TO BUY FROM OR SELL TO CERTAIN BUSINESSES

by closing the port of Boston and placing Massachusetts under military rule, many in the colonies began to argue that they would have to fight for independence from Great Britain. The royal governor of Virginia, John Murray, Lord Dunmore, disbanded the House of Burgesses, which he saw as a hotbed of rebellion. In defiance, the burgesses continued to meet in a local tavern. In the spring of 1774, they resolved that "A Congress should be appointed ... from all the Colonies to concert a general and uniform plan for the defense and preservation of our common rights." All colonies but Georgia agreed to hold the First Continental Congress in Philadelphia in September 1774.

The Virginia House of Burgesses chose delegates from among its members. The Virginia delegates included Peyton Randolph, who was elected president of the congress, and Colonel George Washington. The congress drew up a set of resolutions stating the rights of the colonies to self-government and formed a Continental Association to boycott British trade goods and organize local governments. Finally, the delegates agreed to meet again in May 1775.

Before that date arrived, the first battle of the American Revolution had been fought in Massachusetts. Virginian Thomas Jefferson, future author of the Declaration of Independence, accompanied

Above: Peyton Randolph, Virginian president of the First Continental Congress

Below: The powder storage building at Williamsburg

COMMONWEALTH: STATE OR
NATION GOVERNED BY ITS
PEOPLE; A DEMOCRACY

George Washington to the Second Continental Congress. The delegates voted to raise a Continental Army, with George Washington as its commander-in-chief.

Back in Virginia, the burgesses continued their conflict with Lord Dunmore. In April 1775 Patrick Henry led a group of Virginia militiamen to protest the royal governor's seizure of an arsenal full of gunpowder. Henry forced the governor to pay for the powder. Dunmore then ordered British regulars to occupy the town of Norfolk. A December 1775 attack by patriot militiamen drove Dunmore from the town. The royal governor and his men fled and boarded ships. Dunmore ordered the ships to fire on Norfolk, and the town was destroyed. This action turned most Virginians against Great Britain for good.

On May 6, 1776, Virginians attended a convention in Williamsburg and declared Virginia an independent **commonwealth**. The Virginia delegates then went to the Continental Congress with instructions to propose independence for the thirteen American colonies south of Canada.

The royal governor, Lord Dunmore,
flees the Virginia rebels.

EPILOGUE: MODERN VIRGINIA

Yorktown, Virginia, saw the end of the American Revolution. It was there that the British were beaten for the last time and finally surrendered. After the Revolution, in 1788, Virginia became the tenth state to join the new United States.

Virginia was once covered with forests. Three-fifths, or sixty percent, of Virginia is still wooded. Abundant deer, rabbit, and other wildlife still populate the woods. Virginia's total human population grew from 10,000 in 1645, to 54,000 in 1670, to more than 300,000 before the Revolution, to nearly 7 million today.

Almost three-quarters of Virginia's people live in or around cities. Farming accounts for less than one percent of Virginia's economy. Military bases cover 450 square miles of land in southeastern Virginia.

The more than 20,000 Native Americans who once lived in Virginia have nearly all disappeared. A few small groups live in the southeastern part of the state and in some of the larger cities. They are mostly members of three Algonquian groups: Pamunkey, Mattaponi, and Chickahominy.

By the year 1670, about 2,000 black slaves lived in Virginia. By the time of the American Revolution, in 1775, their number had grown to at least 150,000, about half of Virginia's total population. Today, about twenty percent of Virginia's people are African Americans.

There are many places in Virginia where one can still get a glimpse of colonial life. The most notable of these is Williamsburg, with its original and reconstructed buildings. The Jamestown settlement has also been reconstructed. Several old plantations, such as Carters Grove, can be visited along the James River. George Washington's plantation, Mount Vernon, is open to visitors. The Frontier Culture Museum in Staunton and Explore Park near Roanoke demonstrate how frontier colonists lived in the Shenandoah Valley.

Richmond has been Virginia's state capital since 1779.

DATELINE

APRIL 10, 1606: King James I permits the formation of the Virginia Company, which plans to settle and trade in North America.

DECEMBER 20, 1606: Three ships leave England carrying colonists to the New World.

APRIL 26, 1607: After a long, hard voyage, the English colonists reach Virginia.

MAY 13, 1607: The colonists decide on a place for their settlement, which they call Jamestown.

DECEMBER 1607: Pocahontas, daughter of Chief Powhatan, seems to rescue Captain John Smith from execution by the Native Americans.

SEPTEMBER 1608: John Smith becomes president of the council that governs Jamestown.

WINTER 1609–1610: The Starving Time. Three out of four Virginia colonists die of starvation or disappear into the wilderness.

1612: John Rolfe becomes the first Englishman to grow tobacco in Virginia.

APRIL 1614: Pocahontas marries John Rolfe.

MARCH 1617: Pocahontas dies in England.

JULY 30, 1619: The first elected lawmaking assembly of the English colonies meets in Virginia.

AUGUST 1619: A Dutch trading ship brings the first African slaves to Virginia.

MARCH 22, 1622: Native Americans massacre hundreds of colonists in a surprise attack.

1624: King James I dissolves the Virginia Company and takes over the colony.

APRIL 18, 1644: Native Americans attack and kill several hundred colonists.

1676: Bacon's Rebellion pits the poor colonists against the rich and leads to the removal of the corrupt royal governor, William Berkeley.

FEBRUARY 22, 1732: George Washington is born.

JULY 3, 1754: Virginia militia, commanded by George Washington, a 22-year-old colonel, are defeated at Fort Necessity in one of the opening battles of the French and Indian War.

JULY 9, 1755: British troops commanded by General Edward Braddock, after a march through Virginia, are defeated in an ambush by French and Indian troops.

SPRING 1774: The banned Virginia House of Burgesses calls for a Continental Congress to protect the rights of all the colonies.

DECEMBER 1775: Patriot militiamen force Virginia's royal governor, Lord Dunmore, to flee the colony.

MAY 6, 1776: Virginia declares itself an independent commonwealth.

Glossary

ACT: law, so-called because it is made by an act of government

AMERICA: land that contains the continents of North America and South America

BOYCOTT: agreement to refuse to buy from or sell to certain businesses

BRITISH: nationality of a person born in Great Britain; people born in England are called "English"

BURGESS: citizen of a burg or borough; a representative elected to the lower house of the Virginia colonial legislature, called the House of Burgesses

CHARTER: document containing the rules for running an organization

COLONY: land owned and controlled by a distant nation; a colonist is a permanent settler of a colony

COMMONWEALTH: state or nation governed by its people; a democracy

DUTY: tax collected on goods brought into a country

DYNASTY: series of rulers from the same family, who pass the throne from one family member to another

EMPIRE: all of the colonies under the control of one nation

FRONTIER: newest place of settlement, located the farthest away from the center of population

GREAT BRITAIN: nation formed by England, Wales, Scotland, and Northern Ireland; the term "Great Britain" came into use when England and Scotland formally unified in 1707

INDENTURE: agreement to work for someone for a certain number of years, in exchange for food, a place to sleep, and payment of one's passage across the Atlantic to the colonies

MILITIA: group of citizens not normally part of the army who join together to defend their land in an emergency

NATIVE AMERICANS: people who had been living in America for thousands of years at the time that the first Europeans arrived

NAVIGATION: science of figuring out one's position and direction when traveling on the ocean

NEW WORLD: Western Hemisphere of the earth, including North America, Central America, and South America; so called because the people of the Old World, in the east, did not know about the existence of the Americas until the 1400s

OLD WORLD: Europe, Asia, and Africa

PARLIAMENT: legislature of Great Britain

PATENT: official document giving someone the right to use a piece of land or permission to conduct a business

PLANTER: owner of a plantation, or large farm

POUND: currency, or form of money, used by the British

REGULARS: full-time soldiers in an army

ROYAL GOVERNOR: governor appointed by a king or queen to govern a colony

SHIP'S BISCUIT: hard biscuits that don't spoil easily, taken on long voyages

STOCKADE: series of wooden posts set into the ground, forming a high wall to protect a settlement

SURVEYOR: person who marks boundaries and draws maps of parcels of land, in order to keep records of land ownership

TAX: payment required by the government

WEST INDIES: islands of the Caribbean Sea, so called because the first European visitors thought they were near India

FURTHER READING

Collier, Christopher, and James Lincoln Collier. *The French and Indian War.* Tarrytown, N.Y.: Marshall Cavendish Corp., 1998.

Collier, Christopher and James Lincoln Collier. *The Paradox of Jamestown, 1585–1700.* Tarrytown, N.Y.: Marshall Cavendish, 1998.

Fishwick, Marshall W. *Jamestown: First English Colony.* New York: American Heritage Publishing Co., 1965.

North, Sterling. *George Washington, Frontier Colonel.* New York: Random House, 1957.

Quiri, Patricia R. *The Algonquians.* Danbury, Conn.: Franklin Watts, 1992.

Smith, Carter, ed. *Battles in a New Land: A Source Book on Colonial America.* Brookfield, Conn.: Millbrook Press, 1991.

Smith, Carter, ed. *Explorers and Settlers: A Source Book on Colonial America.* Brookfield, Conn.: Millbrook Press, 1991.

Tunis, Edwin. *Colonial Living.* Baltimore: Johns Hopkins University Press, 1999.

WEBSITES

www.americaslibrary.gov
Select "Jump back in time" for links to history activities.

www.nps.gov/fone/relsites.htm
Find links to French & Indian War-related parks.

http://www.fortedwards.org/cwffa/cwffhome.htm
Explore frontier forts involved in the French & Indian War

http://www.history.org
The site of the Colonial Williamsburg Foundation; select "History" for links to information about the details of colonial life.

BIBLIOGRAPHY

Barbour, Philip L. *Pocahontas and Her World.* Boston: Houghton Mifflin, 1969.

Billings, Warren. *The Old Dominion in the Seventeenth Century.* Chapel Hill, N.C.: University of North Carolina Press, 1975.

Coleman, R.V. *The First Frontier.* New York: Charles Scribner's Sons, 1948.

Duke, Maurice. *Chesapeake Bay Voices: Narratives from Four Centuries.* Richmond, Va.: Dietz Press, 1993.

Hawke, David Freeman. *Everyday Life in Early America.* New York: Harper & Row, 1988.

Middleton, Richard. *Colonial America: A History, 1607–1760.* Cambridge, MA: Blackwell, 1992.

Taylor, Alan. *American Colonies.* New York: Viking, 2001.

The American Heritage History of the Thirteen Colonies. New York: American Heritage Publishing Co., 1967.

INDEX